Because of You
I Live with my
Passions

Because of You
I Live with my
Passions

Di Joseph

authorHOUSE®

AuthorHouse™
1663 Liberty Drive
Bloomington, IN 47403
www.authorhouse.com
Phone: 1-800-839-8640

Published by AuthorHouse   06/12/2012

ISBN: 978-1-4685-8556-8 (sc)
ISBN: 978-1-4685-8557-5 (e)

This book is for my daughter Caroline without whom I would not know the meaning and implications of unconditional love and without whom I would not be who I am today.

Because of you I am Me, Myself, Diana.

Because of you, it does not matter that my book is published or read. It only matters that I have written it and that I have admitted who I am to you and to myself.

I could not have published this book without the support of my brother, sister, my niece and some of my dearest friends. Thank you all for taking the time to review my scribblings and encouraging me to delve deeper. You know who you are. You have read with me, cried with me, prompted me and reminded me that I am more than I think I am. For that I am truly grateful.

Table of Contents

Why?

Did I ever believe that I would just think of a title and then write my book? That may be the way some writers do it but it was not this way for me.

Whenever I thought of writing a book it was a technical text book. That was until the end of 2011 when I realised that I wanted to write a book about you.

I had doubts. Do I have a book in me and if I do, will it be long enough, readable enough, true enough, and sellable enough? Who actually cares? I know I have a book in me but is there enough of me in the book that will interest you? Who cares? That's not why I write this book. I write this book because there is a story in me that has to be told; a story that may resound with you.

As I started to think about my book and what it would contain it became obvious what I would name my book. What's in a name? The title is important because it embodies what the book is about, and it has to do that in just a few words. That's a hard ask. So I tried again and again and again to find a title.

My book is about you; the people, events and circumstances that made me who I am today; the people who affected my life; the events that occurred that influenced my life; and the circumstances which I could have changed. It is not a long story. It is a true story. It is an honest story. Perhaps it could be your story.

Today I am who I am because of you and in spite of you. I am happy in my skin and accept who I am. It has taken me a lifetime to be able to believe this and say it with honesty.

Let me tell you up front that I have an addictive personality. I am also passionate about things. If you can stay with me and read with me perhaps you will draw your own conclusions and see, by comparison, how you have become the person you are.

"The Zulu proverb <u>Umuntu ngumuntu ngabantu</u> expresses a profound truth embedded deep within the core of traditional Afrikan values. It translates into English as "a person is a person because of people." Kwadwo Gyasi Nkita-Mayala.

How true this is for me. I am me because of people.

When I started to write this book it was the start of just another passion, another compulsive act. I threw myself into it heart and soul. I became passionate about delving into my life to understand myself better.

When I had the first draft of my little book ready, I thought 'that's it I've done it'.

But my family wanted to know more and so I started to unpeel the onion. My life, like an onion, has many layers. Some layers are thick, some are thin, each one is a different shade; some layers are easy to disclose, some are more difficult and some must never be told. So I dug deeper. But still they wanted more. The more I revealed the more I understood that there was still more for me to uncover.

I am not able to disclose all the layers of the onion, but I give you a taste of them. Some are sweet, some are strong, some are bitter and some bring tears to my eyes as onions often do.

Because of you I had a Happy Childhood

"Happiest of people don't necessarily have the best of everything; they just make the most of everything that comes along their way." Source: Karen S. Magee

I have wonderful memories of growing up in a poor but happy post World War 2 family. I grew up with love. Let me tell you about how I grew up.

Thinking back on growing up I have uncovered early memories of my need to please, a need of approval, addictive behaviour, a desire to be pretty and my obsession with my weight. It has been eye opening and has explained much of my behaviour over the past 64 years.

I was born in Edinburgh Scotland in November 1947 to my parents Bob and Margaret. We lived in St Stephens Street in Stockbridge. Dad called me the Wonder Child because I could sit at 4 or 5 months. I remind my family frequently that I am the Wonder Child. And they laugh.

My parents also called me the 'Michelin' child because I was so 'roly poly'. Did I perhaps invent muffin tops? I grew out of the baby fat but my weight would haunt me for the rest of my life.

One day, when I was a baby, mum went shopping. In those days there were no large supermarkets. Shopping meant a walk up the High street. Mum left me in my big pram outside the butcher shop while she went inside to buy meat for the day. This was normal practice in Scotland in the late 1940s. When she went home with her shopping, she left me outside the shop. Fortunately a neighbour realised I had been left behind and took me home. Mum was oblivious when the neighbour said she had left something behind at the butcher. She checked her shopping and it was all there. "No I have everything.' she exclaimed. She was horrified to realise that she had left me behind. Well that was mum. Her mind was probably on the cottage pie she would make for dinner when she got home. This story has been told so many times in our family and it is embellished every time it is told. I was left in the snow. I was left in the rain. I was left over night. The family laughs each time the story is told.

I have occasionally thought that this story has given me a fear of being abandoned and so I have held onto things longer than I should have.

Our home had a living / kitchen area with a bed in the recess, curtained off, for mum and dad. Then there was the box room which was my room. There was a bathroom but I am not sure if it contained a bath. I have vague memories of being washed in a large zinc bath in front of the fire. Although it was a basement apartment we had a window at the back onto the grass-less yard where the washing was hung, I spent many happy hours out there looking for bullets and pellets from the war.

I remember the high mantel-piece over the fire. There were 'secret things' up there which I could not reach. Every now and again dad would lift me up so I could look and touch all the 'secret things'. The secret things were probably insignificant things that parents often put out of reach of children. Today I have secret places where I put my private things. Sometimes things are in a box marked private. Sometimes things are placed in a safe. Sometimes things are placed in my handbag. I know they are safe there.

Our family increased when my sister Lindy Lou (Linda) was born and I had to learn to share. I have no recollection of my sister until she was almost 2 years old and I was almost 5. We shared the love of family. We shared clothes as my clothes were passed on to her.

Linda was the 'Beautiful child'. I remember her having straight white hair and a pretty face. She could sulk, was independent, had a mind of her own and was not afraid to show it.

Mum was a talented seamstress and we always seemed to have hand stitched very pretty frocks, hand knitted jumpers and cardigans. We were never without shoes. Despite the hard times we had everything that we needed. We were blessed.

At the age of five in about 1952 I was forced to wear spectacles. I hated them. Each time I looked in the mirror I saw how ugly I was. All we could afford was the round rimmed National Health frames. My school mates called me 'speccy four eyes". I wanted to be the same as all the other kids and instead I was different. Over the years I would hide my glasses so that no one knew I could not see as well as everyone else. Today I am grateful that I can see.

I loved to look pretty and when mum washed my hair she would cover my head in pin curls. The next morning she would remove the pin curls and I would have beautiful wild curls. My love of curls lasted throughout my life. I regularly tortured my poor hair with perms just to have curls. Vanity thy name is Diana.

Growing up, I was a 'good' child and always wanted to please. I remember going to Sunday school from the age of four and diligently learning the text each week. The reward was a small printed text to put in my bible, and of course praise from the teacher.

I remember too that my granddad used to give me a pound if I was first in the class. I worked very hard for this and loved his approval. I have no idea what I did with the money. Recognition was important not the money.

During school holidays, I helped around the house more than most children. I did the shopping, made the beds, set and cleared the table, and washed the dishes. Sometimes I dried the dishes but never the cutlery. To this day I do not do cutlery. I did the housework because I enjoyed and needed approval and recognition. I wanted to please mum and dad.

At school I loved arithmetic and was always chapters ahead of the rest of the class. My handwriting, the result of the dip pen and ink was often held up to the rest of the class to admire. My class mates probably hated me but I didn't notice.

And so began, at an early age, my need for approval. Of all my 'addictions' this is still the hardest to deal with and live with.

We had moved to Ivanhoe Crescent, the Inch, Liberton when our family grew again. The Inch was one of the early council estates and we were very happy there. One of our original neighbours still lives there. The flats were brand new. We had a living room, 2 bedrooms, a bathroom with a bath, a small kitchen and a little balcony. We loved it. I was not ashamed to be living on a council estate. That came later.

My brother Robbie arrived and life was never the same again. Let me tell you why. I was 11 and aware that mum was pregnant. Our school was across the road from our flat and I asked her to stand a book on the window ledge when she went to the Nursing Home. I was very excited on the 6th October 1958 when I saw the book in the window. Dad came home and I remember him singing "It's a boy, it's a boy, it's a bonny bouncing boy . . ." I think he was a little tipsy.

On Sundays I was sent out with Rob in his pram. I had to push the pram till he fell asleep. I would rather have been at home playing in the street with my friends or listening to the adults conversation. I did a terrible thing. I pushed the pram so that Rob's eyes were in the sun so he had to close them. I thought that this would make him go to sleep. I worry today that what I did caused him to have cataracts and that for that I am so very sorry.

Robbie was 'the Golden child'. He was beautiful and had a head of white curls. He cried quite a lot, and so he got lots of attention. We loved our baby brother.

Rob's love of horses started as a baby when he would sit on dads back and they would gallop around our home. Mum could never understand why dad's pockets were always torn. She eventually learnt that dad's pockets were the horse's stirrups.

We children grew up with the freedom to play in the street. I grew up able to fly down the hill when it snowed on a wooden sleigh built by dad. I grew up playing in the street with skipping ropes. I grew up crafting on the pavement. I grew up with children who played in the safety of our street.

I grew up with support from neighbours of our 'sales of work' as we called them where home-made fudge and tablet raised funds for a local hospital. Tablet is hard to describe if you haven't had a Scottish upbringing; *"it's like toffee, but not chewy, it's like fudge, but more grainy. It's basically a wee bit of heaven. (http://scruss.com/tablet.html)"*. In the 'back green' we set up tables and sold everything we had made and collected during the summer school holidays. I was always the organiser of the event. I was a control freak. I loved to be in charge. I loved to organise and I did it well.

In 1960, we donated everything we earned at our 'sales of work' to the Princess Margaret Rose hospital. I wonder if you can imagine 8 probably scruffy children walking into the hospital with about 25 pounds. We were so proud of what we achieved and received a lovely thank you letter from the hospital. I have no idea where that letter is but the words are in my heart. How great it is to do something for someone who needs help. We learnt that at an early age when we had so little.

Our life changed dramatically in 1962 and Rob's love of horses was enabled with a big move. We emigrated from Scotland to South Africa.

It was with great excitement in October 1962 that we arrived at the Waverley Station in Edinburgh headed for South Africa via London and Southampton. I remember that mum and Auntie May cried but we children were so excited. It felt like we were going on holiday. Little did we know that it would be many years till we would see our uncles, aunties, cousins, grandma granddad and friends again.

The "Flying Scotsman" pulled out of the station and took us to London. London is a blur but I remember the train trip to Southampton and then boarding the Union Castle mail ship, the Stirling Castle. I wonder if you can imagine what it was like for our family to board what we perceived to be a 'Luxury Ocean Going Liner'. We were over awed. The next two weeks were the holiday of a lifetime. We swam, we played deck quoits, we looked at the sea, we ate and we slept. We were in heaven.

Things were not so great for mum. She was sea sick and so, spent much of the two weeks in her bunk bed.

Eventually we passed through the Cape Rollers, rounded the Cape of Good Hope and pulled into Table Bay. I have always been an early riser but I will never forget the morning when I first saw South Africa and Cape Town. It was the 18th October 1962 that I climbed the stairs from the lower decks. My back was to Table Mountain and so I was facing Robben Island. I turned around and in front of me was Table Mountain covered in that perfect white table cloth. It is a sight that I will never forget. It is a sight that I have never seen again. We had arrived in our new home.

After we disembarked and cleared customs, we walked all the way up Adderley Street to the Company Gardens. I remember seeing the squirrels. I remember feeding the squirrels. I remember seeing all the young girls in their smart school uniforms. Dominating all my memories was 'the Mountain'. I remember this day in 1962 as though it were yesterday.

But we were not destined for Cape Town. We boarded the 'milk train' and headed for Johannesburg. Our train was called the milk train because it stopped at every small town on its long journey from Cape Town to Johannesburg. It took 2 days to reach Johannesburg. When we arrived we were hot, tired, dusty and just a little grumpy. Johannesburg was very different to Cape Town. There was no sea and no mountain. In Johannesburg there were high buildings and mine dumps.

Mum and Dad immediately found a home for us and then a school for Linda and I.

Linda and I were used to a simple, free, government school so Athlone Girls High School (AGHS) was posh for us. At AGHS we had to wear a school uniform, a Panama hat, black lace up shoes, big green bloomers (not quite panties) which we wore for Physical Education and we had to pay fees just to attend school. I loved it.

Mum and dad struggled to find the money for our school uniforms but eventually Linda and I looked like all the other girls. We struggled to pay the school fees and I was often embarrassed by being called out at assembly because our fees had not been paid. Linda and I were often left sitting outside school because mum forgot to pick us up. When she arrived we all had a good laugh. She worked so hard to make a good life for us and we soon forgot how often we sat on our suitcases outside school waiting for her.

My mother learned to drive at about the age of 38. That is almost unheard of today. She had a funny coloured, old fashioned, second hand Consul named 'Betsy' which she had to drive from home in Rembrandt Park to school in Cyrildene and therefore up the dreaded 'Sylvia pass'—a very steep hill. We used to pretend that we were pushing the car, 'Come on Betsy' we would say, and eventually we reached the top.

Most of my friends mum's drove very smart cars so I was very pleased when we parked un-noticed at the back entrance to the school. And so again my need for approval reared its ugly head. I wanted to be liked and was embarrassed by my poor background; our old car; the very background that had made me who I am.

At school Linda and I stood out like sore thumbs. We spoke with a Scottish accent. The girls loved to hear our accent and were always asking us to speak because we were so different to them. I did not want to be different. I wanted to be like them—rich and pretty. Over the years my accent slowly changed so that I could fit in. I am not sure that I ever did

I became games prefect in my matriculation year, 1965, and enjoyed lots of recognition. I played for the Southern Transvaal schools hockey team, and swam in the swim team. I was allowed to be popular because I was not Head Girl. I wanted to be Head Girl but that was not to be.

The highlight of this last year at high school was the matric dance. The only topics of conversation amongst my school friends were the hair, the dress, the toes, the shoes, the finger nails, the jewellery, the flowers, the car and the partner—the boyfriend.

My mother could always work miracles. She found a beautiful shop in Hillbrow, Johannesburg and there was the perfect dress. It was white and I remember it as Grecian. It fell to just below my knees and the top was draped. I felt like a goddess when I wore it. My long hair was styled in an up-style with big loopy curls all pinned in place. My nails were not professionally manicured nor were my toes. I do not remember wearing makeup.

I attended my matric dance alone without a partner. I was 18 years old and did not know any boys to invite to the dance. I had never kissed a boy. I was too embarrassed to ask my friends if they had a brother or cousin who could accompany me.

Mum and dad drove me to the dance but I did not dance. I was there alone. I remember being very embarrassed. Mum and dad drove me home and I was so sorry that they had spent all that money on my beautiful dress.

My school days were over as was my happy childhood.

Because of you I am a Crafter

"A clear horizon—nothing to worry about on your plate, only things that are creative and not destructive . . ." Source Alfred Hitchcock

Learning to knit is not easy, especially at the age of 4. I remember learning to knit to the rhyme 'In, over, through and off'. With patience, a neighbour sat with me on the back step and showed me how to cast on. She guided me to knit that first difficult row; she taught me how to turn my work; she picked up my dropped stitches. After many tears I eventually learnt how to cast off. This neigzhbour introduced me to a world of making things. This love would eventually grow to a love of yarn, fabrics, colour and texture. She taught me that I could do anything I wanted with my nimble fat fingers.

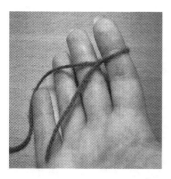

My first crochet hook was my little fat finger. Make a loop tie a knot and place the knotted loop over my finger. Then place the wool over your finger from the back to the front, take the back loop over the front loop. Pull tightish. Then just repeat this process until you have a very long finger chain . . . But what do you do with it when you have finished?

We kids used them for all sorts of things. We tied them to tin cans so we could communicate across our apartments after lights out. We wound and stitched them into little circles that could be used sort of like coasters. We made bracelets and necklaces. We used them to tie up our little brothers and sisters so that they did not escape while we were busy having fun.

When I got my first crochet hook I made blankets and dresses for my dolls. I was hooked. I still make blankets ponchos and even small rugs.

My daughter bought me a beautiful journal where I now record some of my crafting efforts:

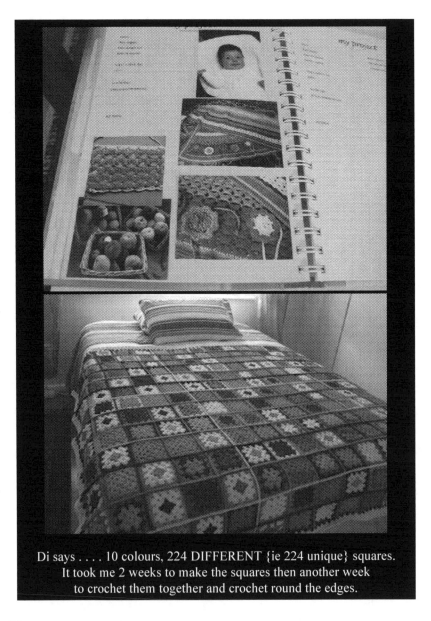

Di says . . . . 10 colours, 224 DIFFERENT {ie 224 unique} squares.
It took me 2 weeks to make the squares then another week
to crochet them together and crochet round the edges.

And of I course I had to weave.

As children, we were very inventive. I remember weaving a little mat for my grandma which she displayed with pride until she died. It sat on top of the television. I looked at it with pride whenever I visited her.

All it takes is a piece of cardboard some wool and a Kirby grip (no not a needle). Cut small grooves in the cardboard at both ends then wind the wool around to what we know is the warp.

We then used whatever scraps of wool we had to weave using our kirby grip to go under and over the warp threads. We did this instictively with very little formal or informal training. Some stuff we just knew how to do. Like birds and fish.

My love of paper, pens and pencils in fact anything you will find in the stationery department was evident whenever grandma took me to Woolworths in Princess Street Edinburgh. We headed straight for the stationery counter and I was allowed to choose a few bits and pieces which I hid at home. I did not always like to use my stash, I just loved to have it. I collected paper, notebooks, pens, penciles, gem clips and glue. I would bring it out to create street projects. I just loved to have it all.

By the age of 5, I was an addict. I was passionate about crafting and paper. It is the one addiction I hope I will never recover from.

It was really my dear mother who I must thank for my love of and passion for crafting. She could do anything, everything and inspired me to do the same. She trusted me with her sewing machine. She encouraged me with my choice of colours and textures. She showed me by example. I am forever grateful that I can tackle any creative project thanks to her. Thank you mum.

When I 'discovered' Kasse Fassett in about 1986 I was a passionate about yarn and knitting and had to share his books with mum. I bought her one of his early knitting books, 'Glorious Knitting' and we created our own glorious interpretations of Kaffe's designs. Mum and I eventually bought so many of Kaffe's books and each had our own collection. 'Glorious Inspiration', 'Glorious Patchwork', 'Glorious Interiors', 'Glorious Needlepoint' and 'Glorious Colour' were the first in our collection. We anxiously awaited his next publication.

Kaffe was and is a truly original and fearless designer who doesn't hesitate to go gloriously over the top.

Mum and I were completely different in our approach to creating. Mum was spontaneous, enthusiastic, quick, a little disorganised and, dare I say it, messy. I was controlled organised and very tidy.

I have a special memory of mum and I working with beads. She was on holiday in Cape Town and we were making sun catchers to hang on the trees in the garden. We were sitting in the garden and each had a tray to work on. My beads were beautifully organised in boxes and the beads were all colour co-ordinated in little compartments. Mum picked up one of the boxes with colours that she liked and tipped them all on to her tray. I tried not to look horrified and mum happily began making her sun catchers scratching through her beads looking for the right colours. I on the other hand carefully looked for the right colour in my compartmentalised colour coded boxes. I finally understood mum's method. She could see the end result before she had picked up a single bead. She saw the beautiful combinations of colours in what I thought was a muddled mess. She worked like a child and was completely uninhibited by whatever constraints I put in her way. Mum's box stayed a mess for her entire holiday and every day she would tip it out and create beautiful little pieces of beadwork. At the end of her holiday she was preparing to organise her box and I had to say "no mum leave it that way for next time". She smiled and hugged me.

I had a similar experience when she I was learning to work with oil paints. First she took me shopping for paint and under her guidance I did not buy every colour in the shop. I bought what she recommended. We bought brushes and canvas. The brushes were of the very best quality at mum's insistence. We bought about 3 for me. Mum had brought her own brushes to Cape Town. When we got home she gave me one of her palettes and we started. I was to copy a still life by Cezanne. We colour washed the canvas so that it was not so white and threatening. Then we started to paint. Mum immediately started mixing colours and soon her white was no longer white. I tried so carefully to mix my colours but hers looked so much better than mine. I realised that I had to be a bit messy. But that was very difficult. I never did fully adapt to mum's joyful and uninhibited technique but I am still trying.

Mum also taught me how to care for and clean my brushes. Her brushes were pristine and looked brand new when she had finished cleaning them. She bought new brushes only because she wanted to, not because she needed to.

Sometimes when mum visited me in Cape Town we would spend a few days whale watching in Hermanus. We would take pencils and sketchbooks and in the afternoon we would sit on the balcony sketching the coastline. I was comfortable with a pencil because I always had an eraser handy. These were the quiet times I had with mum. Mostly she liked to chat and I liked to listen. I miss her.

Because of you mum, I developed a passion for beautiful things. I can admire the great talents of today that are creating in wonderful emerging and innovative styles. Thank you.

Because of you I am a Daughter

"All women become like their mothers. That is their tragedy.
No man does. That's his." Source Oscar Wilde,

What else can I say about a woman who was loving, joyful, spontaneous, impulsive, intelligent, talented, beautiful, 'the life and soul of the party' and my mother?

My earliest memory of my mother is when she spent the weekly rent money for a ticket to watch Margot Fonteyn dance the Firebird with Michael Somes at the Edinburgh Festival in 1954 in Edinburgh. I was 6 years old. I am so glad that she did this. I wish that she had bought 2 tickets and taken me with her. My mother was impulsive and seized opportunities to do wonderful things. When I was about 19 mum came home from work and told us she was going to Thailand for the long weekend.

Mum's friends called her Mags, Maggy Rush and Maggy Tea.

Her work friends called her Mags. Mum was passionate about her work and she worked hard to provide for her family. She made a success of everything she tackled. She did not always know what she was doing but she hid it well. And she was successful. My sister, brother and I inherited her passion to work.

We kids called her Maggy Rush. When mum wanted to do something she did it and there was no stopping her. I remember coming to visit and she had bought a new house. She did not consult with dad. She just did it. And so the old house was sold, she moved into the new house and then rushed about changing things. She was handy with tools. When she wanted an archway she got out her sledge hammer and started to break down the wall.

Mum's Scottish friends called her 'Maggy Tea'. Now I wonder why that would be. Mum loved food and particular she loved cake and sweet treats. When we were out for dinner, she read the menu from the back focusing on the desserts. I remember going to Sun City with family friends,Moira Jeanie,

Laurie and Moira's mum. We had dinner in a very posh restaurant. When the dessert trolley arrived it fell down the stairs and all the beautiful desserts fell off the trolley and onto the floor. We all reacted in the same way. 'Oh no there go the Maggie Teas'. Mum would have been horrified.

My dad called her Margaret. It was her name. It was the name of the woman he married. It was the name of the mother of his children. I do not remember him calling her anything but Margaret.

I called her Mum when I was able to talk to her. My sister and brother are outgoing extroverts like Mum. They chat easily. They make friends easily. They socialise easily. I have always been more introverted like dad. But I wanted to be like mum. Mum could make a party happen. Every new year we had a Hogmanay party. Hogmanay is the Scottish word for the last day of the year and is synonymous with the celebration of the New Year. Mum would prepare Black bun, pies, sandwiches and lot of wholesome food that would keep our revelers relatively sober till the new year was welcomed into our home. Just before midnight a tall dark haired guest would exit our home carrying a piece of coal and a bottle of whisky. He would be our 'first foot', the first person in our home for the New Year and would surely bring blessings and good luck.

When the music started it was mum who would start the dancing. She would work the room bringing together couples and making them dance. Mum's parties were memorable. No one misbehaved and no-one got outrageously drunk. Everyone just had loads of fun. Eventually in the wee hours of the morning when all the guests had left, we kids would start to clean up. We discarded old drinks, bottles, food and scrubbed the floors. When mum and dad woke up the house was back to normal.

If I could change any relationship I have had, it would be the one that I had with Mum. I have regrets. I could have treated her gentler. I could have treated her as an adult. I could have confided in her as a mother. I could have just spoken to her. I could have shared my happiness and sadness with her. I could have just listened to her without getting impatient. I could have spent more time with her. I could have. I could have. I could have. It's too late now.

If I am envious of my sister it is because Linda had a more honest relationship with my mum. This was probably because she spent more time with her over many years. At the end, my dear sister took mum every day for her radiology treatment to treat an incurable brain tumour. My sister bathed my mum, dressed her and helped her into and out of the car. My sister encouraged my mum to eat and swallow her 'smashing' medication. Linda and mum sat at the Johannesburg General Hospital from the early hours of the morning until it was time for mum's treatment. On the 14th February 2005, my mum died. She died in my sister's arms and for that I am eternally grateful. She died in the arms of unconditional love. I was not there.

If all women become like their mothers then what I most fear is that my relationship with my daughter will be the same. That is not remotely good enough. Is there time to make it better and to fix it? I hope so.

My dear mum if I could just have another chance with you. My dear Caroline if I could just have another chance with you.

Because of you I love scrambled eggs

"The secret to making moist, fluffy scrambled eggs is all in the scrambling. You'll need low, gentle heat and patience to make perfect scrambled eggs."

All my life I did not eat breakfast. I know that it's the most important meal of the day but growing up being extremely weight conscious I believed that as long as I delayed eating I would not gain weight and as long as I devoured the appetite suppressants this was true.

Not eating was just another of my many addictions. I deprived myself the joy of eating in order to stay slim. I have no idea what damage this caused me, but looking back, this is just another indication of my addictive personality. I swallowed 'diet pills' for years. They were expensive but I could not do without them. I think they were 'uppers' and they got me through the day.

My treat at home was when my father made me scrambled eggs. He whisked the eggs until the whites disappeared. He added some milk and black pepper and then cooked the eggs in a pan with a little butter. The eggs did not stick to the pan. They were delivered on a slice of hot buttered toast and presented to me for breakfast or dinner. When I lived away from home and came back for business Dad would ask me what I would like for dinner. I would say scrambled eggs. That is what I got. Perfect. My father cooked eggs for me just the way that I liked them. He scrambled them. He disguised the bits that I did not like (the whites) with the bit that I did. He beat them up till they were light and fluffy and served them on hot buttered toast.

Because of my father I understand that I can disguise what I do not like with what I do and make that acceptable. Because of my father I love scrambled eggs.

I remember visiting Johannesburg and staying with mum and dad. Dad asked me what I was doing in Johannesburg and I told him I was attending a training course. He looked at me and gently asked "What can they possibly teach you?"

He was so proud of his 3 children. I know that he had incredible confidence and faith in me and truly believed I was one of the best. I wish I could have shared that confidence but I always believed I was not good enough. He also understood my addictive personality. I was not clever enough. I was not pretty enough. I was not popular enough. I was not good enough. I was just not enough.

It's now 2012 and I am in my mid 60's I have defeated some of my food addictions and I now love Eggs Benedict. A muffin halved and toasted smothered with salted butter, crispy bacon, topped with two soft poached eggs then smothered with Hollandaise sauce sprinkled with a dash of cayenne pepper then finally some freshly ground pepper. Now that is what I call breakfast. I still cut off the egg white.

My father was the gentlest, kindest and most generous man I have ever known. His primary goal in life was to care for and provide for his family. He did a great job and his legacy to me is so much more than scrambled eggs.

> "... I've made it my business to observe fathers and daughters. And I've seen some incredible, beautiful things. Like the little girl who's not very cute—her teeth are funny, and her hair doesn't grow right, and she's got on thick glasses—but her father holds her hand and walks with her like she's a tiny angel that no one can touch ..."
> Source Adriana Trigliani

My dad was a quiet person. He rarely raised his voice and he did not talk much. He saved his voice for when he had something valuable to say. I remember him driving me to work and often we would say nothing the whole trip. We did not have to talk.

When I moved to Cape Town in about 1987 things changed a little. Every morning from Monday to Friday he phoned me at 6.00am. He never missed a day. We spent about 2 minutes on the phone just checking that we were both ok. Dad would ask if I had anything planned for the day other than work and normally the answer was 'no dad, just work today'. I looked forward to his call.

I have looked for my father in every man I have ever met but have never found him.

Because of you I was a Wife

"Only two things are necessary to keep one's wife happy. One is to let her think she is having her own way, and the other is to let her have it." Source Lyndon Johnson

In 1972 at the age of 25 I was married. But my love affair with love started 5 years earlier. I seemed to meet men who wanted to marry me. Or perhaps I persuaded them that they wanted to marry me. Or perhaps it was the era. I was engaged to Don, Fred, Tommy, Chris, John and finally Lambros.

I seemed to lurch from one 'serious' relationship into another. I was in love with the idea of being in love and being loved. I was addicted to love. When I think back I felt no remorse in breaking off my engagements. I just moved on to the next one.

When I met Lambros (at work) I was engaged to John. Lambros swept me of my feet with his bubbly effervescent personality.

Let me help you visualise Lambros. He was 5 foot 8 inches tall, and had long curly blondish hair. He had blue eyes. He had a smile better than and wider than Julia Roberts' smile. When he smiled his mouth met the little wrinkles on his eyes. He was gorgeous and he loved me. He was wild, drove a big motor bike and was unlike anyone I had ever met. He was loud and popular whereas I was quiet, shy and retiring. He was of Greek descent. There was no getting out of it with Lambros and so we were married.

1972 was a time of plenty. We started our life together in a lovely apartment; we bought a new Alfa Romeo, a big motor bike; and our maid Lena helped us maintain our home. We holidayed several times a year in Durban and the Drakensberg.

Life was good but it was noisy and turbulent. Lambros had a temper. Being Greek he did not share the chores around the house so I became a house keeper as well as being employed full time.

I would always do anything for peace so Lambros bought a new car and bike every two years. He had a passion for music and musical equipment so we had a whole wall filled with enormous hi fi equipment. As fast as he turned up the volume I turned it down and he turned it up again and I turned it down. We lived on a rollercoaster.

Lambros loved his motor bikes. The first time he went to the army for the compulsory 3 month training exercise, he prepared carefully. He went down to the garage and drove his 750cc Honda motor bike into the lift where he stood it on the back wheel. He then rode the bike along the passage into our home and parked it in our enclosed balcony on the 7th floor of our building. There it sat till his return. No, I did not wash it or polish it. I ignored it for 3 months.

With both of us working we were not short of money.

Lambros and I did have some fun times. I remember our honeymoon spent at Drakensberg Gardens hotel in Kwa Zulu Natal. We were young and energetic and joined in every activity offered by the hotel. We played bowls in the morning; we rode horses in the afternoon; we sat on the balcony and waited for the bell to ring for afternoon tea; we 'dressed' for dinner; we played darts after dinner. We made friends. It was all very colonial, and I loved it.

But my relationship with Lambros was volatile and I prayed he would 'calm down'. No such luck. He never did while we were married. He had a temper that sometimes resulted in him injuring himself, and then there would be peace for a while.

Lambros was a jealous man and very possessive. He hated if anyone looked at me. I used to walk with him with my eyes down just in case I glanced at someone. I remember walking in Sandton City and he blew his top because he thought someone had looked at me in an inappropriate way. I should have worn a yashmak. He was so handsome that I should have been the jealous one. He loved to flirt with all the girls.

However during our marriage I was the one who was unfaithful to him. It was 1977 and I was attracted to a man who worked with me. When my husband went off to the army for another 3 months compulsory training I had an affair. The affair was short lived. I had to change jobs. I started to smoke.

When Lambros came home from the army I had to confess to the affair, show him I was a smoker, tell him I had changed jobs and finally confess I had bought a car without his permission because I had to drive to the new job. He was devastated and angry but forgave me. Or did he? What I did was unforgiveable. What kind of a woman would do that to her husband especially when he was defending the South African borders? Well I did. I was thoughtless, selfish and egotistical. I thought only of me. I did not understand or consider the consequences. I have no excuses.

My unreasonable search for love, approval and for 'me' would be my downfall.

In about 1979 Lambros suggested that we could save a lot of money on income tax if we were not married. He suggested we divorce secretly. I had become used to doing what he wanted and so I agreed. And so unbeknown to friends and family we were officially divorced. I believe now that both he and I saw this as our escape when the time came.

I had a great job with S.P.L. at this time of my life. I worked in Sandton City and with my new found freedom, my car, I had some independence. This was not to last. Lambros came home one day very angry and very determined. He had had a fight with his boss (his cousin) resigned and told me we were moving to Durban. I was horrified. Firstly my work and family were in Johannesburg. Secondly, I did not like Durban. I could not bear the heat and humidity and, Lambros' family lived in Durban.

I had a love hate relationship with Lambros' very strong family. Although I loved his mother dearly she was a domineering and manipulative woman. The thought of being so close to the Greek side of the family filled me with fear.

My inability to say 'no' became evident and I looked for a way to procrastinate. I thought that delaying tactics might work so we agreed that I would move 3 months later. This never happened. I was free and so was he.

Looking back over the years I realise now that if I had invested as much time and energy in my relationship with my first husband as I did with another relationship, Lambros and I would not have parted. But this is hindsight. After we parted Lambros fell in love with Vanessa and had two beautiful children Nina and Chloe. We are all blessed.

My beautiful 4 year old daughter Caroline became the pawn. But again, I am moving too fast. Let me tell you about Caroline and being a mother.

Because of you I am a Mother

"The moment a child is born, the mother is also born. She never existed before. The woman existed, but the mother, never. A mother is something absolutely new." Source Rajneesh

When Lambros and I decided to have a child I secretly prayed for a girl. Everyone was convinced that I was having a boy. I did not want to tempt fate so I decorated her room in white with just a touch of blue. All of the clothes I made were white. I made sheets, pillowcases, blankets, matinee jackets and bootees all in white. Mum, Linda and I shopped for Cantley baby grows—all in white and all bought from Stuttafords in Sandton City Johannesburg.

I inherited maternity clothes from my sister and had a carefree pregnancy with no problems and no morning sickness. I remember that first movement and my baby wriggling around. I can still see that little foot kicking out reminding me that she was there. I worked until 5 days before Caroline was born. I then got stuck into washing blankets and spring cleaning as I have heard that this is what lots of mums-to-be do. It kept me busy for at least 4 of these days.

Giving birth was not so easy LOL. I was in labour for about 24 hours before they decided to do a caesarean section. I regained conscious in my room and sent a nurse to find out what my baby was. "It's a girl" came the answer. I sent another nurse with the same request. "It's a girl" came the answer. I did not believe them till they placed Caroline in my arms and I was able to check for myself that she was a girl.

As we mothers do, I un-wrapped my baby and counted fingers and toes. Her nails looked like she had just had a manicure. To this day she has beautiful manicured nails. I touched her face, that perfect skin and her little body. To this day she has beautiful skin. She was perfect. I did not check that she was a girl. I just knew. My prayers had been answered. She was perfect and beautiful. Oh I hear you say all babies are beautiful. Caroline was beautiful on the day of her birth and she is today.

I have only had 1 child but I know that Caroline was exceptional. She ate and she slept. When she was awake she smiled and gurgled. She was contented. I was a blissfully happy mother.

Caroline was born with a mop of black hair. When we brought her home from the Nursing home a neighbour looked at us all in the lift and asked—so where did she get that black hair?—Both Lambros and I were blondish. This became part of the story "Tell me about when I was a baby". Caroline loved this story and I would tell her in detail of how I had prayed for a girl, how I had decorated her room and made clothes for her. I would tell her of the night before she was born, the day she was born, the man in the lift, and how she met her family. I could tell her the story in the same way 37 years later.

My addiction to Caroline had begun.

It has taken many years to get over the guilt of giving custody of my daughter to her father. I did what I thought to be the right thing at the time.

When Lambros moved to Durban, Caroline moved with him. I settled into a small cottage in Illovo. My brother Rob and his friend Harry helped me paint the cottage, and soon it was home. Every second week I drove to Durban to see Caroline. We spent wonderful weekends at Chaka's Rock, Beverly Hills Hotel and Umhlodti beach. Caroline loved the beach and would spend hours collecting shells and living creatures.

Eventually I took Caroline back to Johannesburg. We found a school for her to attend and I tried to settle into a single parent routine. But I had met Mike. But again I am moving ahead of myself and Mike is another chapter. I gave custody of my daughter to her father and took her back to Durban. To this day I do not understand why I did this. But I did.

It was about 1 year later that I was speaking to Caroline and she said she wanted to live with me. I was overjoyed. I told her I would discuss it with her father and see what we could do. When I spoke to Lambros he was furious. He told me that we would go to court and Caroline could tell the judge who she wanted to live with. I could not do this and so I told Caroline her father's decision. This made Lambros even angrier. He could not believe that I had told Caroline what he had decided.

I escaped from Lambros to protect myself. However I left my daughter under his control.

I am not sure that my daughter understands this because she loves her father. As she should. Unfortunately I could not love him unconditionally and realised that I had to leave him in order to survive. And survive I did.

I cannot unpeel any more of this onion. It is too personal and cannot be shared.

Because of you I love my Work

Growing up I wanted to be a school teacher. I was inspired by some great teachers in primary and high school. I cannot remember all their names, but I do remember Miss Benson, my mathematics teacher. Thank you. Numbers were my passion. I remember that when I was a child and had pneumonia; I suffered from a fever and numbers danced around in my head making patterns. Numbers kept me awake. Numbers, formulae understanding how they worked has driven me; I wanted to be a mathematician but was not talented enough.

When I matriculated I enrolled at Teachers Training College in Braamfontein Johannesburg and was sent to the University of the Witwatersrand (WITS). I did not do very well at University probably because I did not always attend my lectures. What I enjoyed was sitting in the canteen with a cup of coffee, discussing anything, everything and solving world problems.

My second passion was computers. So I dropped out of University and went to work at Leo Computer Bureau in Johannesburg in 1967 where I learnt to 'program computers'. I discovered my next addiction—work.

I grew up in the very early days of computers, systems design and technology so there is nothing in this IT profession that frightens me. I just love it. I am now able to combine this love with my desire to teach by conducting training courses.

But I am moving too fast.

I started work at the age of 13 delivering newspapers morning and afternoon. It was 1960 and I loved being employed and getting paid for working. I earned 15 shillings a week for working just a few hours each day from Monday to Saturday. I got up early (at about 5.00am) and walked to the Newsagent. There I picked up my papers and packed my bag. Saturday was pay day and my friend and I bought 2 ounces of 'smarties' as our pay day treat. My 15 shillings was spent on all sorts of special things.

Occasionally I would ask my sister to do the Saturday afternoon paper round so I could go to town and shop. I paid Linda 2 shillings and sixpence but it was worth it.

My next job was working in a clothes / haberdashery local shop in Cyrildene Johannesburg. It was the end of 1965 and I was 18 years old preparing to attend university. This job too was lots of fun and I earned R10 per week. I remember the owner of the shop making us bagels for lunch. The bagels were laden with smoked turkey and cream cheese. We normally had 2 each. I loved food.

My salary was enough to buy clothes for my next year at university. With my R10 I could go to Woolworths in Hillbrow and buy a top, skirt and sandals. Some weeks I would buy fabric and sew dresses to boost my university wardrobe.

My next job in 1966 was waitressing at a steak restaurant close to the university. I have no idea how much I earned. But I remember making a double thick chocolate malt and a hamburger at the end of my shift. Working in a steak restaurant was not easy. I came back home to residence smelling of food, cigarettes and alcohol. But in those days we did what we could to supplement our pocket money. My parents could not afford to subsidise my entertainment. I did not expect them to.

And then my life time career started. Throughout the rest of my working life I have been blessed. To love your work is an amazing gift.

In 1968 I was employed as a junior computer programmer and my obsession with work started. I earned R190 per month which was such a lot of money in these days. My mentors were Tony Van Zyl and Judy Gantor. Tony was our manager, and Judy was an exceptional Analyst. They both inspired me to be the very best.

Dad drove me to work and I was normally there before 7.00am. I was like a sponge anxious to learn everything about computers, how they worked, why they did not work and how to design systems that would stand the test of time.

I had arrived. At last I could afford to contribute to the family. I gave mum R50 per month. This made a huge difference to her budget. By this time my sister was also working and she did the same. It was the time of plenty. Today, it is hard to imagine that just R100 per month could make such a significant difference to the way we lived. But it did. Again we were blessed.

In 1968 computers were enormous. They normally took up a whole floor in huge buildings. No laptop on my desk. I had a program specification, 'coding sheets' and 'punched cards'. The days flew by and eventually I knew what I was doing. 3 years later I was ready to move on to my second job.

In 1971 I became a programmer at OK Bazaars in Johannesburg.

A big advantage in starting my career in the early days of computers is that I grew with all the wonderful changes in technology. I worked with the early methods of designing and implementing real time computer systems. I grew with data base technology. I grew with 4th generation programming languages. I grew with the World Wide Web. I grew with HTML. I grew with web enabled computer systems. There is nothing new today that remotely scares me. I am still growing.

Addicted to work it was late one night that I met my first husband, Lambros. In those days I thought nothing of working all day then all night then all the next day. I was young, strong and needed little sleep. And I loved it.

Great opportunities came in 1977 when I moved to my 3rd job at S.P.L. based in Sandton City. My years at S.P.L. were the golden years of my career. I worked with some of the most talented systems people I have ever met. I had the opportunity to work with exciting technologies and exciting people. My addiction to work increased. Working at S.P.L. was like working with a family. I remember we had a kitchen and a fridge full of drinks. We ran an honour system. If we took anything from the fridge we wrote it on a sheet which was stuck with a fridge magnet to the fridge. The system worked because we were all honest. Nothing went missing from the fridge.

Such good days. I remember some of the very special people who influenced the rest of my career; Len Israelstam, Trevor Winer, Geoff Evans, Lewis Folb, John Gardiner, John Raymond and Hettie Steyn. These colleagues were the best of the best and I was privileged to have known and worked with them.

In 1981 desktop computers (for business) were emerging and I seized the opportunity to start my own company and sell my own software. My mother was working for Hewlett Packard and she needed software to sell these desktop computers known as the HP85, HP86 and HP 87. I worked night and day developing standard business packages such as payroll, salaries, accounts receivable. I was 34 years old and unstoppable. As mum sold the computers so I would sell the software. Selling software packages was the bread and butter. Custom built software for me was the jam on top. I was a designer and developer and I worked night and day.

Linda, my sister, joined me to do the installation and support and she was phenomenal. Soon she was selling stationery and all sorts of consumables to our customers. This left me free to develop enhancements to the software and build new packages.

It was during this time that I met Mike. Much of my work time was dedicated to building a system for him. He also bought all of software packages. My addiction to work was combined with my addiction to Mike. What a combination.

When Mike and I parted I re-joined S.P.L. and a new chapter of my life began. But again I am moving too fast. Let me tell you about Mike.

Because of you I have Loved,
been Loved and Cried

"If you love something set it free if it comes back its yours
if not it was never meant to be" Unknown

I met the love of my life, my soul mate in 1981 and my life would never be the same again. Michael was married and I had no intention of breaking up a family, a marriage and a home. But I did. I contributed to it.

Mike and I met through work, my other addiction. I went to his office one Saturday to discuss his requirements for a tendering system he wanted me to develop. I knew from the moment I met him that I was helpless. He was like a magnet attracting me to him mentally, physically and spiritually. He was hypnotic.

I have to believe that we were in love. There was no space for friends, family or children. It was all about the two of us—for a while. We were selfish and self-absorbed.

It was Christmas 1981 and Mike gave me a beautiful solitaire diamond ring. I assumed at the time that this was an engagement ring. I put the ring on my ring finger. In retrospect perhaps I was wrong. I do not remember him asking me to marry him. I assumed that a diamond ring meant an engagement and marriage.

Mike and I married in the garden of our townhouse in Johannesburg 1982. I organised the wedding in about 3 weeks. About 50 close friends joined us to celebrate our wedding; I wore a beautiful Laura Ashley dress and felt like a princess. Our girls and my nieces all had Laura Ashley dresses and they looked perfect.

Mike and I had some good times. We travelled to Australia and sailed around the Coral Sea. We travelled to the Caribbean and sailed around the British and American Virgin Islands. We travelled to London. We travelled to the Isle of Man.

Michael travelled overseas on his own for business about 2 weeks out of every 4. So perhaps we did not spend enough time together to really work on our marriage. When Mike was home his two daughters would come to spend weekends with us but Mike was normally working so did not spend much time with them. I enjoyed having Victoria and Charlotte to stay. We would play make believe games. We chatted and laughed. We rented a 3 bedroomed townhouse and furnished bedrooms for them. Victoria had her own room and Caroline and Charlotte shared. I have not seen the girls since Mike and I divorced. I just abandoned them.

One day we were living together. One day we were married then one day we were divorced. I never understood how all this came about in such a short time. I have a mental block about how long this took and when it happened, I cried bitter tears. I cried angry tears. I cried tears of regret. I cried tears of longing. I cried for a long time.

Mike and I lost touch for almost 20 years but he was often in my thoughts. He moved to the United States and I moved to Cape Town. Mike visited Cape Town occasionally. When he did we would meet and I was filled with guilt and shame. Was Mike married during this period? I do not know. I never asked and he never told me. I felt like I was dangling on a string and he could reel me in whenever he felt like it. Eventually I said 'no more' and cut the string. We lost touch for many, many years.

I was working in Durban in January 2010 when Mike found me through Facebook. He contacted me, we talked and all the emotions resurfaced. I was overwhelmed at the sound of that same gentle voice. We met briefly a few months later and it felt like time had moved backwards. I felt the same love. I wanted to just walk into his arms and put the clock back to relive it all again.

We tried to talk about what had happened but it was difficult. We both had different memories of what had happened, who did what and who said what. Why did we marry? Why did we divorce? We had more questions than answers. Perhaps one day if it is still important we will understand what happened and why.

Mike has remarried, is happy and a changed person. We both know that our happiness cannot be obtained at the expense of another's.

Mike is erratic again about staying in contact. I thought that I had reconnected with a friend but when I send short SMS's just hoping that he is well, I get no response. This is fine. I can now keep in contact without expecting him to respond. However I cannot help thinking that perhaps he is not well and is unable to reply.

After all these years I still love Mike but am not in love with him. I know that we cannot be together. My comfort is in knowing that our love was mutual all those years ago. It is good to know that I have loved and been loved.

Because of you I allowed myself to be Used

After Michael I thought I would never smile or laugh again. I became the ice queen, frozen in a state of distrust, fear, misery and anger. I could not understand that with all that love and passion Mike and I could not make it work.

As usual, work came to the rescue. I re-joined S.P.L. and was placed for a few months in Cape Town. Although I loved Cape Town I made no friends until my last day. I met Will and he made me laugh. He was nine years younger than me. I was 39 years old.

I returned home to Johannesburg and my dear mother saw the change in me and rejoiced. I had moved out of the Michael Misery. I will always remember Will phoning me the day I arrived back in Johannesburg and he made me laugh. Mum was hovering in the background with a huge smile on her face.

About 4 months later I had the opportunity to relocate to Cape Town and I took it. I never intended for Will and I to live together so quickly but we did. He just seemed to move in and take over my life. We had a few good years and tears.

In 1987 it was with great excitement that I bought my first home. It was a double storey semi-detached Victorian townhouse in Tamboerskloof Cape Town. I was 39 years old. I fell in love with the front door. I had wanted my own home ever since my marriage to Lambros so I seized the day and bought it. Will lent me R7000 for the deposit and I paid that back many times over the next 20 years in blood, sweat and tears. Will and I moved in and although he was working he did not contribute one cent to our living expenses. In my head I deducted monthly expenses from the loan but perhaps that was wrong. Did he want the R7000 back in one lump sum?

I loved living in Tamboerskloof. I had a house that was big enough to accommodate guests and a small garden where I could begin to get to grips with the earth. My tiny garden became a sanctuary. I bought a Victorian bath which became the plunge pool! Caroline loved to cool off in the bath on hot Cape Town afternoons.

I sanded doors to reveal the beautiful yellow wood. I sanded the stair case then painted it again because it I believed it was not good enough to disclose the bare wood. It was my first house. I owned it. I loved it.

We bought Finlay our beautiful Scottish Terrier and it was thanks to him that we eventually moved to the suburbs. Neighbours complained that Finlay barked all day so we decided that he needed a garden

When I sold the Tamboerskloof house we moved to Tableview and this time Will and I bought our house together. This was my big mistake because Will put nothing into the house. No money and no effort. Moving to Tableview in 1989 with my dear maid Margaret I learnt to garden.

My garden became my escape and my return to the soil. I loved to get my hands dirty. I spent many hours at the garden centre buying plants, seedlings and compost. When I returned home it was with great pleasure that I dug in the compost, created new beds and planted my seedlings. Gardening physically exerted me. Gardening made me dirty. Gardening helped me see the wonder of the circle of life and death. Gardening was my escape.

For whatever reason, Will stopped working and I became the sole provider. I became the enabler. For peace I would do and pay for anything. I have no idea what he did all day. Alcohol played a big part in his life. There were so many embarrassing situations but our friends just seemed to accept it. I accepted it. Will was a binge drinker. He did not drink at home unless we had friends over.

It was in November 1997 for my 50th birthday that Will and I travelled to Vietnam. Will's brother Gordon lived in Saigon so this became our base for the holiday. Gordon and his partner Rosemary made us very welcome in their beautiful home. From Saigon we travelled inexpensively by bus using 'Sihn Café' to the Mekong delta. Vietnam was completely different to everything I had ever experienced. It was brown and green and every now and again there was the most beautiful flower in the most obscure of places that lifted my spirit. I loved it. It reminded me of hitch hiking in Spain in the late 1960's. It reminded me of the poverty of my roots. It reminded me of the joy of my childhood. It reminded me of just how much I have to be thankful for.

After the Southern Mekong Delta trip, we travelled North to Na Trang and I was grateful for the coolness of the northern highlands of Vietnam. The green ness of the coffee plantations is incomparable to anything I have ever seen. From Na Trang we travelled East to CaNa on the South China sea. It was here that I left my heart. As soon as I stepped of the bus I knew I had to stay. Can you imagine the enormous smooth boulders, sitting in that muddy coloured sea? I wanted to stay. I wanted to take my suitcase off the bus. I wanted to rent a cabin on the beach. I just wanted to spend time there.

But what will Gordon say? What will Rosemary say? I stood at the side of that bus and allowed myself to be persuaded to 'get back on the bus.' And I did. Gordon did not give a damn. Rosemary did not give a damn. Will did not give a damn. I have cared for many years.

This was the time of my life when I cared too much about what people might be thinking about me. Guess what they are not thinking about me. They were not looking at me and judging me. If anything they just may have been looking at themselves and wondering what I was thinking of them.

Many years of my enabling destroyed Will's self-esteem. He did not have to work. He had a housekeeper and his own personal bank. This is when I should have learnt tough love. As long as I had my work I could survive. As long as I had my work I had the money to enable him not to work. Perhaps I am being too harsh on myself because I did encourage and pay for him to do a course in tourism. He seemed to enjoy it, but when the course and study was over he did not get a job.

When Will was good he was very, very good, but when he was bad he was horrid.

When I eventually asked Will to leave in in 1998 he went to Thailand. I had to buy his share of the house from him and off he went. He was there for two weeks spent all of his money then asked if he could come back. The 'No' word escaped me. I allowed him to come back.

It was another 5 years, 2003, before he left my life again. This was the last time. Again, he went to Thailand and I have no idea what he did, how he lived but he survived.

I spent 15 years of my life in a relationship that was going nowhere. Eventually we arrived at nowhere.

Will came back to Cape Town in about 2008 after I had relocated to Johannesburg and we communicated regularly. He seemed to have changed. He was sort of self-supporting.

When it was time for me to relocate again, this time, back to Cape Town in 2011 I asked Will to fly to Johannesburg to drive down to Cape Town with me. We had a great trip back. He was sober. Can you understand that I still cared for him? Settled in my new apartment in Tableview I would invite him to have soup, bread and cheese with me. He was sober. He did not ask me for anything. I gave him only a meal every few weeks and some company I thought that I had put the past behind me and still had Will as my friend. It was not to be.

The wheels finally fell off on December 28th 2011. I am forever grateful to my brother Rob who escorted Will from my apartment. Will was drunk, abusive and out of control. What he did, what he said and how he behaved in my home was unforgiveable. My brother did what I could not do.

Will called the next day and said he was sorry. I could only reply "Sorry doesn't it cut this time Will". With these words I closed a door on 24 years of my life. I have no regrets.

Will used me, abused me and stole from me. I allowed it. I begin to forgive myself for being the enabler. If only I had exercised tough love . . .

I forgive myself for what I did to you Will, I will forget what you did to me, but I cannot forgive what you did to my family.

Because of you I am 'Other Mother'

After Lambros and I had finally decided we would never live with each other again, we were both lucky enough to find another love.

Lambros and Toby went to school together in Zululand and were very good friends. Vanessa is Toby's sister. Lambros and Vanessa fell in love and married. I was very happy for them both but hoped that Lambros had matured and softened a bit. They had two beautiful daughters Nina and Chloe. Nina looks just like Vanessa and Chloe looks just like her father.

Caroline lived with her father and now had two sisters. The girls all loved each other so much. I did not have too much time with Nina and Chloe. When their father died tragically I travelled to be with the family in Durban. It was then that, in her grief, I was able to talk to Vanessa to thank her for being 'other mother' to Caroline.

I remember asking Vanessa to treat Caroline as though she was her daughter not a step daughter. It could not have been easy for her but she did a great job for which I will always be grateful. I always hoped that I could do something small in return for Vanessa, Chloe and Nina.

A few months after Lambros death I heard that I was the beneficiary of a small policy which he and I had taken out in 1972, the year we were married. Rightly or wrongly I assumed that Vanessa and the 3 girls had been taken care of. However I sensed some animosity when discussing the policy with the executers of the will. My problem was solved when I remembered that Lambros had promised Caroline a car which she had not received. When I decided to fulfil this promise to her by buying her a car with the proceeds of the policy, the animosity fell away. I bought a blue Beetle for Caroline and this was her father's gift to her as promised.

My opportunity to give something back to Vanessa came in 2007 when my sister Linda, brother in-law George, Nina, Chloe and I travelled to England for Caroline's wedding.

Nina and Chloe arrived in Johannesburg from Durban and I arrived from Cape Town. Chloe had an unfortunate accident before leaving Durban and her foot was very badly damaged so our trip started with a wheelchair. We were all escorted quickly through passport control because of Chloe's wheelchair. From there we went to the Premier Lounge and the girls had great fun helping themselves to whatever drinks and food was on offer.

It was an easy trip to London and there to meet us were Caroline, Stuart (Caroline's fiancé) and Danni (my niece). We had about 5 days to the wedding and there was a lot to do. We did it all.

The girls did not like the dresses Caroline had selected so we all went to Welwyn Garden City. I remember leaving Nina and Chloe while I went off to find a wheelchair. Instead I got a little electric car and Chloe's face was a treat when I drove it round to her. She thought she was getting a wheelchair and she had such fun driving around the shopping centre. We found perfect dresses for Nina and Chloe. At the same time we bought fascinators for all of us. We had great fun trying them on.

Two days before the wedding Caroline realised that she did not like her dress. She was in tears. 'No problem' says I let's go shop! So back we went to Monsoon and bought her a beautiful dress.

On the day before the wedding we all had pedicures. Chloe had a mini manicure as well because she only had one foot on show.

We had a week of pampering. This was a very special time for Caroline. She had her sisters all to herself and could spoil them.

The night before the wedding we stayed in a hotel close to Great Wymondley. Danni had made hen party packs for us and after a few drinks we were all in party mode. We had a ball. We did the song from 'First Wives Club' 'You don't own me' and Nina and Chloe were in hysterics. I remember them saying, "you taught us how to party!"

I had a wonderful time with Caroline Nina and Chloe—three sisters and I really felt like 'other mother'.

After the wedding we spent lots of time all together. We visited Camden. We shopped. We laughed. We lived. Thank you Vanessa for sharing your girls with me.

Because of you I have Power Today

"God, grant me the serenity to accept the things I cannot change,
Courage to change the things I can,
And wisdom to know the difference."
Source Reinhold Niebuhr.

The Serenity Prayer is the common name for an originally untitled prayer which has been adopted by Alcoholics Anonymous and other 12 step programs.

It was on the 6th of November 2008 that I called Alcoholics Anonymous (A.A.). I wanted my life back. I did not analyse if I was an alcoholic and in fact family members denied that I was. All I knew was that I wanted to stop drinking alcohol. And so one day at a time I did. I attended meetings. I studied the Big Book. I studied the 12 Traditions.

I worked the program in my normal addictive way. I was addicted to A.A.

The preamble to A.A meetings (this is read at the start of A.A Meetings around the world) says it all:

"Alcoholics Anonymous is a fellowship of men and women who share their experience,
strength and hope with each other that they may solve their common problem and help
others to recover from alcoholism.
The only requirement for membership is a desire to stop drinking."

Step 9 of the A.A. 12 step program says:

"Made direct amends to such people wherever possible,
except when to do so would injure them or others."

There are things that happened in my life that I cannot confess to. There are people I have hurt that I cannot make amends to. These are the things I live with each and every day. That is the price I pay and I willingly pay that price.

In writing this book I give up my right to Anonymity. I share my life willingly with you.

Sharing my 'anonymity' with individuals that I am friends with and work with has brought me great rewards. I have been able to share my experience with people who are not alcoholics but suffer from the effects of other addictions. For that I am grateful.

My message is to <u>anyone</u> who suffers from any <u>addiction</u>. There is hope and there is help. I reach out my hand to help you. All you have to do is grasp it and I will hold on tightly. Just want to help yourself and you will help me too. I need you to continue to grow in my recovery.

It is not enough to commit to A.A, for someone else. It had to be for me. The 3rd Tradition of AA says *"The only requirement for A.A. membership is a desire to stop drinking."* This was and is my only requirement. The first step of the A.A program says *" "We admitted we were powerless over alcohol—that our lives had become unmanageable."* This is all that it takes to get started.

But eventually I wanted my power back. I no longer wanted to be powerless.

I do not know how or why I relapsed. But I did. Did I lose track of 'one day at a time'? Did I become complacent? Did I stop going to meetings? Did I stop meeting with my sponsor? Yes to all of the above. The disappointment for Caroline was, I can only imagine, unimaginable. I did not know how much my drinking affected her.

It took me quite a while to get really back on track. I no longer have to label myself as an 'alcoholic' or 'recovering alcoholic'. This is not who or what I am. No I am not in denial, I just have a desire, right now, today to stop drinking. That's enough for now. But if I do have a drink I am no longer powerless. That's enough for today.

I am not just an alcoholic and do want to be labelled as such, I am passionate. I am a worker. I create. I live. I have friends. I shop. I love my life.

I still use the steps and slogans as they have become a part of who I am but I am no longer "religious" about it. I don't attend meetings; I am no longer mainly defined by the fact that I am an alcoholic. I am me, I have learned a lot and I can say with confidence that I will never be part of a co-dependent relationship ever again.

Because of you I know
the Love of a Sister

"If a man does not keep pace with his companions,
perhaps it is because he hears a different drummer."
Source Henry David Thoreau

My sister Linda "marches to her own drummer". She is confident, clever, strong, opinionated and honest. She works so hard then comes home to work some more. Yes, she is sometimes an ostrich burying her head in the sand. Eventually the head peeks out and she faces the reality. She is my little sister and whether she likes it or not she will always be my little sister.

"Did you ever know that you're my hero,
and everything I would like to be?
I can fly higher than an eagle,
'cause you are the wind beneath my wings.'
Source: Jeff Silbar and Larry Henley

My beautiful sister is my hero. She was and is 'the Beautiful Child' and I cherish every day we have to spend together. She is my best friend. But that was not always the case . . .

Linda had to walk in my 'goody goody' shadow at high school. I was a people pleaser and rarely put a foot wrong. Linda was her own person. She was in fact my mother. She was outspoken and accepted the consequences. She was honest.

I remember an episode from about 1967. Linda, Rob and I were fooling about and they tied me up hands behind my back and feet tied together. They rolled me on to my hands and knees then pushed me over. My face crashed down onto the carpet. I like to say that this is my excuse for having a funny nose but I think I was born with the funny nose. My nose was so sore I thought it was broken. We all laughed. I was 20 at the time.

I was envious of my sister for all sorts of reasons but mostly because she is just perfect.

My dear sister Linda,

> "*. . . You're simply the best, better than all the rest*
> *Better than anyone, anyone I've ever met . . .*"

My sister makes me think of all my favourite stars; Bette Midler, Tina Turner and Meryl Streep. She is all of them wrapped into one. She is everything I would want to be. I am blessed that she is my sister and part of my life.

When I retired from work at the end of 2007, I sold my house in Cape Town, packed up some of my treasures and moved to Johannesburg to live with Linda and George.

I settled into life in Johannesburg and retirement. Linda and George were both working so I was able to help a little by doing the daily shopping and getting dinner ready to prepare. I set the table and had coffee ready for Linda when she got home from work. And I crafted; sewing, crotchet, knitting, card making, and scrap booking. I was bored.

During the last 10 years Linda and I have become particularly close. And by that I only mean that we have spent more time together and we talk more on the phone when apart. She makes me laugh till my jaws ache. Every now and again she can still make me cry. I remember the last time she made me cry.

It was the 28th November 2011. I had relapsed from my A.A. program a few months before. We were in Johannesburg; Linda, George, Danni, Caroline and I. For some reason some flippant remarks at the dinner table got out of hand and an ugly argument ensued.

The discussion started with lots of joking and laughter. Caroline explained that I always buy a hard nail brush when I visit her in Hertfordshire. We all laughed. I have to brush my nails and for some reason never take one with me on trips. I buy a nail brush whenever I travel because I like my nails to be scrubbed. Then we moved on to face cloths. I buy them whenever I travel. We all laughed. They did not know why I use face cloths. I use them to dry my dentures after cleaning them. I told the girls that they should throw out everything I leave behind after my trip. When I have guests to stay whatever they leave behind I throw out. Then the conversation moved to my driving. OK I have only been driving for 35 years so they are allowed to criticise. We all laughed.

Then the conversion moved to tomatoes. Have I told you that I do not eat tomatoes? 'I buy 2 tomatoes'; no 'I buy 3 tomatoes'. It was the final straw. My reasoning was that I buy tomatoes in Woolworths and they sell them in packs of 6 or 8. It was all so very silly, but I was hurt, embarrassed, and I exploded. No one laughed.

Why on earth would I tell you this silly story? Simply because I exploded.

I sometimes feel that people around me are allowed to be angry and aggressive, but I am not. I sometimes feel that people around me are allowed to joke but I am not. I sometimes feel that people around me are allowed to be sensitive and I am not. I sometimes feel that people around me can say what they want but I cannot. I sometimes feel that I have to live by a different set of rules.

A few hours later Linda came to my room and eventually said she thought I should go back to Alcoholics Anonymous (A.A.) meetings. It was so very hard for her to say these words. I cried. She did not believe that I was an alcoholic but she knew that attending A.A meetings was good for me.

A.A. meetings help makes me calm. A.A meetings give me the Serenity to accept the things I cannot change. A.A meetings give me the courage to change the things I can. A.A. gives me the wisdom to know the difference. A.A keeps my mouth closed. I sometimes think that A.A. keeps me dishonest because I cannot say the things I want to say.

Alcohol gives me the courage to say things I believe in but I lose my Serenity. Alcohol lets me think I can change the things I cannot change. Alcohol removes the wisdom.

My sister knows me warts and all. My sister loves me warts and all. My sister forgives me warts and all.

My dearest sister I hope that I die before you because I would not want spend my last days without you.

Because of you I understand Tough Love

"The Man In The Glass

When you get what you want in your struggle for self,
And the world makes you king for a day,
Just go to a mirror and look at yourself
And see what the man has to say.

For it isn't your father or mother or wife
Whom judgment on you must pass,
The fellow whose verdict counts most in your life
Is the one staring back from the glass.

Some people might think you're a straight-shootin' chum
And call you a wonderful guy,
But the man in the glass says you're only a bum
If you can't look him straight in the eye.

He's the fellow to please, never mind all the rest,
For he's with you clear to the end,
And you've passed your most dangerous test
If the guy in the glass is your friend.

You may fool the whole world down the pathways of years,
And get pats on the back as you pass,
But your final reward will be heartache and tears,
If you've cheated the man in the glass.

Source Unknown"

I have a need for approval. And so I find it difficult to say no. I am and have been the enabler in several co-dependency relationships. I have always found it easier to pay for peace.

This poem helped me. I imagined my brother looking in the glass and he did not like what he saw. And I was seeing his and my reflection and I did not like what I saw.

In my thirties Rob, his friend Harry and I spent some great times together especially between my relationships. They would take me shopping and encourage me to buy loads of great clothes. The age gap between us was less noticeable and it was really cool at 34 to go shopping with two 24 year olds. Rob always had great taste so my shopping trips always ended with loads of stylish clothes and big dents in my credit card.

However when Rob and I went to dinner together I was embarrassed. I thought that people were thinking that he was my toy boy. How silly.

Around this time Rob asked me to help him with his finances. I did. He would bring me his salary at the end of the month in cash. And I would divide it up into envelopes; One each for rent, petrol, food, and weekend entertainment. We budgeted based on the number of weeks in the month. Every Monday I would give him the budget for food and petrol and every Friday I would give him the budget for entertainment. It worked well.

For about 15 years Rob lived independently, and successfully. He worked hard. He bought homes and he lived in comfort. He was always pedantic about his home. It was immaculate. It was clean. It had style. His animals were well trained and well behaved. It was a joy to visit his home. But. Things changed.

Over the years I became an enabler. For those of you who do not know, an enabler is a person who enables another person to persist in self-destructive behaviour (such as substance abuse or financial dependence) by providing excuses or by making it possible to avoid the consequences of such behaviour.

I enabled Rob by giving him money when he needed it. This did not happen overnight. It was over a period of over 15years.

What was the final straw for me? I was always vulnerable to Rob's pleas for money and while I was working it was easy. However I was no longer working. I had joined A.A. I had begun to understand co-dependencies and the fact that I was an enabler. I remember that he called me one day and needed quite a lot of money. Not quite able to say no, I told him that I would pay for the last time but suggested that he did not contact me for a while. I was desperately unhappy that I had brought him to this because I believed it was my fault.

I received a call immediately after Rob's call from an A.A. friend. He asked me to share at an A.A. meeting. It was a life saver for me. It was during this time that my life went out of balance in a different direction. I became addicted to A.A. and the 'Big Book'.

It took me a long time to accept that I was an enabler and then I had to do something about it. Rob and I got to a stage where I was helping to destroy him. It was then that tough love had to step in and tough it was for all of us. I was 63 and he was 53. My sister and I bought him a ticket to England and convinced him to go. He was on his own. No family support system, missing his son, relying on friends for accommodation and trying to pay his way. I threw him into the lion's den.

18 months later I am so proud of him. He has recovered his dignity and self-respect. He works, he saves; he is a responsible adult. He pays his way and he works hard. He can look in the mirror and like what he sees. When I look at him, I love what I see. When I listen to him, I love what I hear. I am blessed.

Tough love is not to be taken lightly. Tough love is not for sissies. It sometimes takes quite a while to face up to the fact that tough love is the only answer. Tough love works for everyone concerned in the intervention if you commit to just how tough it will be.

Because of you I know Friendship

"Be slow to fall into friendship; but when thou art in,
continue firm and constant." Source: Socrates

Sue and I met in 1967 and have now been friends for 45 years. In those days we met every day. We ate breakfast together—toast with apricot jam. We travelled to University together. We attended some lectures together and we travelled home together. We chatted we giggled we gossiped and we laughed. I had made my first friend.

Sue and I spent our pocket money at John Orr's buying fabric, threads and trimmings. We loved to sew. Saturday was sewing day. If we had a date for Saturday night then this day was dedicated to making a new outfit.

When our children were small, Sue and I spent a lot of time together but as our lives changed we drifted apart. Real friendship is forever and despite the times we have spent apart, whenever we get together the years slip away and we are those same 20 year olds. Our connection is 45 years deep and nothing can change that. Sue and I drifted apart after Lambros and I parted and she was not part of my life with Mike.

Although my relationship with Will ended on a sour note it's thanks to him that I met my Cape Town girlfriends. I met the girls in 1987 and they were all about 10 to 15 years younger than me. At 40 I felt so old, old fashioned prim and proper. But our relationships have changed, matured and deepened over the years. I count my blessings that I have in my life, Di, Jill, Wendy, Sheila and Samantha.

I have participated in Christenings, watched the children grow up, attended birthday parties and am comfortable that I am Auntie Di. The age difference between my Cape Town friends and I does not worry me anymore. It diminishes as we all get a little older. As with all my friends we do not see each other often. We chat on Facebook and when there is an occasion, we celebrate together.

At about the same time in 1987, in the S.P.L. offices in Pinelands Cape Town, we were short of space. A new recruit Morag shared my desk whilst I spent time at a client site. The moment we met I knew we would be lifelong friends. We worked together on the ADAPT project at BP in Cape Town. We laughed together. We worked long hours and I learnt about the creative Morag. I met Morag's family and friends. We were together at BP when I shared the news that Morag would be a grandmother to James.

It was while working with Morag that I earned the name 'propeller head'. She was the great business analyst / designer and I was the techie. We worked so well together. Morag was so good at the detail and I was good at the big picture. We were an awesome team, we were a great combination and I spent so many happy days working with Morag.

Morag and I left S.P.L. and were working together at Sanlam when I had to buy half of my house from Will. It was about the year 2000. Morag lent me the money to give to Will until the bond was completely transferred to my name. I will never forget this act of unconditional friendship and love. She just did it with no fuss and no questions. If I remember correctly there was no written agreement. We just trusted each other.

I neglected my friendship with Morag for several years but know that when we meet again the years will slip away and the old memories will return.

And then there are my pub friends, Linda, Little Di and Noel. I met Little Di in about 1992. She was working in our new local pub, the Royal Oak, and we became instant friends. A few years later Noel joined our little group and then came Linda who now owns the pub. Our friendship survives despite minimal contact. We are just friends. Little Di is called 'Little Di' because she is shorter than I am. I am 'Big Di'. When people meet me they cannot understand why I am Big Di because I am almost 5 foot two inches. We all socialised at the pub and had wonderful impromptu parties together. Little Di and I fell out for a short while but after a few months we realised how foolish we were behaving. We forgave each other and the incident was forgotten.

When Little Di left Cape Town to be with her family in England it was Noel and I who took her to the airport. We said our farewells but we all knew that it was not good bye. See you soon dear friend.

I met Shelley at Old Mutual In 1998 thanks to my dear friend Jeremy. My work life took another wonderful turn. Shelley is a perfect perfectionist. She demands exactly what she expects of herself and that is the highest of standards. I have never been able to achieve these standards but I continue to try.

Thanks to Shelley I had wonderful opportunities to grow. I worked with Anne Marie and we built an awesome system. But let me first talk about Anne Marie. It was thanks to Shelley that I met AMB and we met through similar circumstances to how I met Morag. I borrowed her desk while she was on leave. When she came back she was not pleased and I had to move. When we started to design our generic data quality measurement and correction system, AMB was not convinced. But she persevered with me. One amazing day the penny dropped and she understood my systems design principles. I was enchanted! AMB's enthusiasm and dedication grew and she came up with brilliant ideas to grow our design. We called our system 'GENA' which stood for Generic Application. It is the best and last system I have ever been part of. I would love to build another system but time and opportunities are running out. I am proud of all the systems I have built and been part of but GENA was the best.

Working with Shelley, I was given the opportunity to attend and present papers at International Data Quality conferences. Thanks to my passion to please I loved being on the podium and enjoyed the recognition. Thankfully, I never forgot that I was representing Shelley and our team and that my words were a combined effort of that dedicated team. Every presentation I gave was quality assured by a team committed to delivering the best.

My relationship with Shelley has always been professional yet she is my dear friend. It's not always easy to keep the two separate. It's like we each wear two hats and are always aware of which hat we are wearing. I wish I could wear the friend hat more often.

So Shelley, Because of You I slowly become the person I was meant to be. I can accept criticism and advice. I hate to disappoint you in my work and do strive for that perfection. Thank you for being the role model that you are.

My daughter Caroline introduced me to the 'new' form of scrapbooking in 2005. I was hooked. I had made scrapbooks all my life. I made inexpensive scrapbooks using photographs, cuttings from magazines and newspapers, but this form of scrapbooking used completely different resources. It was expensive. The new form of scrapbooking appealed to my creative and obsessive instincts. I could buy loads of stash.

Returning home to Cape Town I attended a scrapbooking class and met Roz. We became friends immediately. Roz is extraordinary. She is flamboyant, outrageous and extravagant. She also has an obsessive personality. We spent many happy days and nights together, scrapping, smoking and drinking.

I remember the Christmas when we 'tired of Christmas'. It was November 2007 and I had just sold my house in Tableview Cape Town. I stayed with Roz until I flew to London to visit Caroline and Stuart. We were working on lots of Christmas scrapping projects and played Boney M all day and all night. We made wreaths. We made angels. We made cards. And we made more mini wreaths. I sipped wine and Roz sipped whatever she was sipping. It was a great time for the two of us. We spent all day together and much of the night.

This was the last time Roz and I had so much time together. I moved to Johannesburg after my London trip and many things would never be the same again.

I am not sure that I am a good friend, but I love my friends. I do the best I can. My friends accept me as I am and I accept them as they are. We forgive each other. We are tolerant of each other. We are friends.

"The most beautiful discovery true friends make is that they can grow separately without growing apart." ~Elisabeth Foley

Because of you I am growing old in a new South Africa

I was 15 years old when I left Scotland to come to South Africa with my family. I knew nothing of apartheid or racial discrimination. I learnt quickly enough. I became part of the privileged minority and for that I am grateful. Although I understood being poor I had no idea of the real poverty that so many South Africans suffered from. I grew up in a 'whites only' society and it was only when I attended university that I began to understand what this meant to many millions of under-privileged black people. But it was with blinkers that I ignored the fate of so many people. I got on with my life.

I remember asking my parents what they did about Hitler. They did nothing. I do not blame them for this, although I did as a teenager. I remember wondering how I would answer my daughter if she asked 'What did you do about Apartheid in South Africa?' I did nothing substantial.

Times eventually changed, as they do.

Nelson Rolihlahla Mandela, (born on the 18 July 1918) served as President of South Africa from 1994 to 1999. He was the first South African president to be elected in a fully representative democratic election.

I do not remember the violent times after Mr. Mandela's release from prison. I only remember a feeling of hope that eventually things would change.

It was at Ellis Park in Johannesburg on the 24th June 1995 when South Africa defeated the New Zealand rugby team that I felt the tides turn for a free democratic South Africa. Nelson Mandela wearing a Springbok rugby shirt and cap, presented the Webb Ellis Cup to the South African captain Francois Pienaar. And 40 million South Africans celebrated.

At this time, I lived in Tableview Cape Town and on the 24th June 1995 the area was silent. No traffic no people walking about. It seemed as though everyone was at home or in the local pubs watching the rugby. I am not a rugby fan but even I watched the rugby in the Royal Oak.

I had made a large colourful poster with the word of "Nkosi Sikelel' iAfrika" so that we could all sing "Lord Bless Africa" at the beginning of the game. Our pronunciation was probably not very good but we sang with gusto.

"Nkosi Sikeleli Africa
Malup hakanyiswu phando lwayo
Yiswa imithanda zo yethu
Nkosi Sikelela
Thina lusapo lwayo

Enoch Sontonga 1897

Things changed that day for many people. We saw an entire nation behind the Springbok team. Mr. Mandela did many great things but that day he made an incredible start at uniting all the people of South Africa.

But change does not just happen. People affect change.

Because of you I am Me

"Obsessive–compulsive disorder (OCD) is an anxiety disorder characterised by intrusive thoughts that produce uneasiness, apprehension, fear, or worry, by repetitive behaviors aimed at reducing the associated anxiety, or by a combination of such obsessions and compulsions. OCD sufferers generally recognize their obsessions and compulsions as irrational, and may become further distressed by this realisation." Source Wikipedia.

I suffer from the disease of alcoholism. This is me. It is no one's fault. It is not because of you. I am an enabler. This is me. It is no one's fault. It is not because of you. I was addicted to over the counter drugs. This is me. It is no one's fault. It is not because of you. I have an addictive personality. This is me. It is no one's fault. It is not because of you.

I am probably mildly obsessive compulsive if that is possible. I certainly fit the definition.

But there is another me. There is the me that that interacts at work and with friends. There is the me that makes me who I really am. This is the me that I see when I look in the mirror. I am not just a recovering alcoholic. I am not just OC. I am not just a people pleaser. I am not just an enabler. I am not just someone who has difficulty in saying no. I am so much more than that.

Apart from everything you have read about me there is another me. I am mostly kind and generous. I love my friends. I can laugh at myself. I am grateful for what I have and how I have lived. I love life. I am still impulsive.

If I could choose I would be dressed by Dame Vivienne Westwood and drive a Marauder or perhaps a Beetle.

I dress myself and so I choose to dress simply and mostly in white. When I shop if I see something I like I buy 2 or 3 or more of the same thing. I buy clothes that are soft and float. The fabric must wash well. If it does not I throw it out. Cotton, linen and muslin are my favourites—in that order.

I do not buy many expensive clothes, but every now and again I buy some good classic pieces that I can use to dress up my cheap clothes. It works well.

I buy lots of white cotton drawstring trousers which I wear under and with everything. I wear them with sarongs and dresses and every year I discard the well-worn ones and buy new.

I dress appropriately for my age. I would hate to be perceived as 'mutton dressed as lamb'. Yes I still care about how people react to the way I look. So I wear nothing too clingy and nothing too revealing. I care about the way I look and of course love accepting compliments about my style. I have a style.

I love high big platform shoes. They make me feel taller than my 5 foot two inches. However the older I get the less often I wear them. My brother Rob detests wedge shoes. I hide them from him. I think that secretly he knows I wear them.

Old age is not for sissies. The knees are not so flexible, I cannot walk as far as I would like, my body shape has changed and my face of course shows the evidence of a life in the sun. Wrinkles.

But there have been some good things with age. I now spoil myself.

I have my hair done every week at 7.00am on Saturday mornings. My dear friend Natalie is the best hairdresser ever and I let her do whatever she wants. We let it grow, we cut it, we colour, we change the colour we make the hair smooth and we make it spiky. We try not to get bored with look.

I have a manicure and pedicure about every 6 weeks and I have a facial once a month. About 3 times a week I give myself a feet treat—exfoliator foot masque, and overnight foot cream. This takes about 30 minutes and its great relaxing time.

A little pampering is good for me and I wish I had done this many years ago. It makes me feel good about myself. It makes me feel that I am worthy of the pampering and me time. It allows me to relax as I was never able to in previous years.

No I do not have another addiction! But if I do, it's a good one and it's good for me.

I have smoked for more than 30 years. I did not sneak a cigarette behind the bicycle sheds at school. I started in my very late 20's. I do not always enjoy my cigarettes. I could save a lot of money if I stopped smoking. I know that it is bad for me. I know that it makes me smell. I know that it is bad for my health. I try not to let it affect your quality of life. Until I have decided to stop for my reasons I will smoke.

I love beautiful things! Sometimes I buy impulsively just because it says 'buy me, buy me'. I buy things that I do not need but know I will love to look at; beautiful plates that remind me of oriental carpets; beautiful fabrics that feel like oriental carpets and beautiful carpets that are oriental carpets.

I have an addictive impulsive personality and this is not going to change. It's too late for that. It's who I am. It's the result of the life I have led.

But I have not stopped growing. I am the person I am today because of you. I will never stop changing. I will continue to be affected by you, the special people in my life. Some of you are no longer with me in body but are with me in spirit. Who will I be in 5 or 10 years' time? I am sure that I will be a better version of the person I am today.

I have bared most of my soul to you and to me. I have cried some tears along the way. I have relived things that that were previously hidden. I have no more that I can share. Can you accept me as I am? Can you accept the person that I am Because of You?

Accept Me As I Am

If you cannot accept me the way I am
Then kick me out your life and tell me scram
As you can't reshape the branch of full grown tree
So take me as I stand or let me be.

I know in my own way I do act strange
But I am way beyond the years for change
So accept me as I am or bolt that door
And shut me out your life forever more.

You say I'm distant when your friends are about
But there's a time for speech and for shut mouth
And I should have thought that you already knew
That never speak until you are spoken to.

And though I do confess I love you true
I'll not be changing not even for you
I could not change my personality
By doing so I could fool no one but me.

I cannot alter my mentality
So accept me as I am or set me free
I could not live a lie or be a fake
So I cannot change not even for your sake.

Accept me for what I am the one you know
Or either set me loose and let me go
As it's not my fault I am the way I am
For after all I'm just a common man."

Francis Duggan